Rethink Revolution

Unleashing the Power of Fresh Perspective

By

Jeremy E. Ayala

TABLE OF CONTENTS

INTRODUCTION

In a world that is always changing, our capacity to adapt and prosper depends on our readiness to question accepted wisdom and reevaluate our viewpoints. This is "Rethink Revolution: Unleashing the Power of Fresh Perspective." This book is a call to action to transform the way we approach the intricacies of our lives and thoughts, not only an investigation of them.

We set out on a trip that goes beyond the bounds of common thinking in the next chapters.

The pages herein serve as a witness to the transforming force that comes from accepting novel ideas, challenging preconceived notions, and widening our brains to consider previously uncharted territory. We learn about the unrealized potential that resides in the desire to question the status quo as we explore the complexities of this rethinking revolution.

Get ready to be led through anecdotes, reflections, and useful tactics that will enable you to overcome the limitations of habitual thought. Together, we'll negotiate the uncharted territory and open doors to creativity, invention, and personal development.

"Rethink Revolution" is more than just a book; it's an invitation to enter a universe where new insights become the motivation behind your path to achievement, contentment, and a life well-lived. Now let the revolution start.

SECTION ONE

The ability to know things you don't know

Knowing what you don't know may be a great tool. It can assist you in learning new things, avoiding mistakes, and developing yourself. You're more inclined to look for knowledge and ask inquiries when you are aware of your ignorance. This can broaden your knowledge and help you discover new things. Because you'll be more inclined to double-check your work and make sure you're doing things right, it can also help you avoid making mistakes. Being aware of your ignorance might also make you more receptive to fresh ideas and open-minded.

Being conscious of your own limitations increases your likelihood of being receptive to new ideas and willing to attempt things. You may develop personally and become more well-rounded as a result of this. Being open to learning new things and conscious of your own limitations are essential for success in life. It's empowering to know what you don't know, and it may help you accomplish your objectives. Here are some pointers for understanding your ignorance:

* Have humility. Never hesitate to acknowledge your ignorance. Everybody has knowledge gaps, and it's acceptable to not be an authority on everything. Make inquiries. Ask someone who knows something if you don't. Asking questions is the only way to learn, and there's no shame in not knowing anything.

* Conduct research. Make an effort to learn more about something by conducting research. Libraries and the internet both have a wealth of resources. * Remain receptive to fresh perspectives. Never be scared to take risks or pick up knowledge from others. You'll become more aware of your ignorance as you gain more knowledge. It's powerful to know what you don't know. It can assist you in learning new things, avoiding mistakes, and developing yourself.

The value of having an open mind to new concepts

One of the most crucial traits someone may have is the ability to be receptive to new ideas. It enables us to advance both intellectually and professionally.

It also fosters our ability to be more inventive and creative. It's crucial to remain receptive to new ideas for a variety of reasons. It first enables us to develop and learn. We are more likely to be exposed to fresh knowledge and viewpoints when we are receptive to new concepts. This can help us in our quest to increase our knowledge and comprehension of the world.

Having an open mind helps foster creativity and innovation. We are more likely to generate original concepts and solve issues when we are receptive to fresh ideas. Both our personal and professional lives may benefit from this.

We may increase our chances of success by being receptive to new concepts. It is more crucial than ever to be able to pick up new skills and adapt to changing circumstances in today's fast-paced world. We may do this by being receptive to new concepts.

Having an open mind to new concepts might only improve your quality of life. We are more likely to come up with fresh and intriguing conversation topics when we are receptive to new experiences. We also have a higher chance of making new friends and meeting new individuals. Openness to new ideas can be fostered in a variety of ways. Being more conscious of your own biases and prejudices is one way to go about it. We are all biased, even if we frequently aren't conscious of it.

Being conscious of our prejudices allows us to begin challenging them and to be more receptive to new ideas. Increasing your curiosity is another way to become more receptive to new concepts. We are more inclined to look for new knowledge and experiences when we are interested. Additionally, we are more inclined to be receptive to novel ideas. In addition, it's critical to have a risk-taking mindset. We are more likely to attempt new activities and encounter novel concepts when we are prepared to take chances. Although it might be frightening, this has a lot of rewards. It is possible to learn and improve the talent of being receptive to new ideas. Gaining this ability will help you live a more prosperous and fulfilling life.

Here are some more pointers for widening your mind to new ideas:

*Show that you are prepared to listen to others. Pay close attention to what other people are saying when you are speaking with them. Even if you disagree with their viewpoint, try to comprehend it.

* Stay receptive to criticism. Reject criticism from others without becoming defensive. Instead, make an effort to understand what they are saying and take something away from it.

* Show openness to trying new things. You will never learn anything new if you do the same things over and over again. Try something new and venture outside of your comfort zone. Have an open mind to change. There will always be change.

You will fall behind if you are not adaptable. Accept change and use it as a chance to improve.

*Show curiosity. The secret to learning and development is curiosity. Inquire, investigate novel concepts, and never give up learning. Being receptive to new ideas is a continuous process. It is a worthwhile trip that can result in a more prosperous and satisfying existence.

What confirmation bias can do to you?

The propensity to look for, analyze, concentrate on, and retain information in a way that supports one's beliefs is known as confirmation bias. It is a systematic inductive reasoning mistake and a form of cognitive bias.

Individuals exhibit this bias when they choose to believe only the facts that confirm their opinions, rejecting the facts that contradict them, or when they read the unclear facts to confirm their own beliefs. Deeply ingrained views, emotionally charged concerns, and desired results are the ones where the influence is highest. Relationships, decision-making, and problem-solving are just a few of the areas in life where confirmation bias may cause issues.

It may aid in the dissemination of false information and conspiracies. There are several strategies for lessening confirmation bias's effects. It is important to be conscious of prejudice and actively look for data that defies preconceived notions.

Another is to weigh all viewpoints before making a choice.

Here are some instances of confirmation bias in action:

* An individual who thinks that vaccinations cause autism may only look for evidence to support their theory, disregarding or ignoring alternative data.

* A person in a relationship with infidelity may only see the instances in which their spouse betrays them; they may overlook or downplay the instances in which their partner shows them love and support.

* A person who thinks a certain political party is dishonest could only watch news outlets that confirm their views, rejecting or ignoring those that offer an alternative viewpoint. Because it can cause us to make bad judgments, confirmation bias can be a harmful kind of prejudice. It is critical to recognize this prejudice and take action to lessen its influence on our daily lives.

The following advice can help lessen the effects of confirmation bias:

* Recognize the prejudice. Becoming conscious of confirmation bias is the first step towards mitigating its effects. As soon as you recognize the prejudice, you may begin to search for strategies to prevent it.

* Look for material that challenges your assumptions. Seeking information that defies your assumptions is one method to lessen the effects of confirmation bias. This might be challenging, as it can be unsettling to question our own views. But it's crucial to keep in mind that the only way we can be certain our views are accurate is to expose them to different points of view. Take into account various viewpoints. A further strategy to lessen the effects of confirmation bias is to weigh the opinions of several people before making a choice. This entails hearing what other people have to say, even if you disagree with them. It also entails having an open mind to the potential that you may be mistaken.

* Remain flexible in your thinking. Lastly, it's critical to maintain an open mind in the face of fresh information. This might be challenging, as acknowledging our mistakes can be an ego-deflating experience. But it's crucial to keep in mind that being receptive to new ideas is the only way to develop and learn. One strong cognitive bias that may significantly affect our lives is confirmation bias. We may make better judgments and strengthen our connections if we are aware of the prejudice and take action to lessen its effects.

The advantages of critical thinking

The capacity to reason logically and coherently while making decisions about what to do or believe is known as critical thinking.

It encompasses the capacity for introspective and autonomous thought. In order to succeed in school, the workplace, and life, one must be able to:

* Understand the logical connections between ideas; * detect inconsistencies and common mistakes in reasoning; * evaluate the credibility of information sources; * synthesize information from multiple sources; * construct and defend a position; * communicate effectively. It aids in decision-making, problem-solving efficiency, and preventing deception by others. * Better decision-making is one of the advantages of critical thinking. By assisting you in weighing the advantages and disadvantages of many possibilities and understanding their pros and cons.

Critical thinking may help you make better judgments solving issues. By assisting you in determining the problem's underlying cause, coming up with potential solutions, and weighing the advantages and disadvantages of each one, critical thinking may help you solve issues more successfully.

* A critical evaluation. You can detect prejudice and propaganda and assess material critically with the use of critical thinking.

* Originality. Your ability to think creatively and generate original, cutting-edge ideas may be enhanced through critical thinking.

* Interaction. By improving your ability to listen to and comprehend people, speak properly, and organize your thoughts, critical thinking can help you communicate more successfully. * Self-knowledge. You may increase your level of self-awareness by using critical thinking to recognize your own prejudices and presumptions.

* Individual development. By assisting you in being more open-minded, adaptive to change, and capable of learning from your mistakes, critical thinking may help you develop personally. There are a few things you can do to enhance your critical thinking abilities:

* Practice. Your ability to think critically will improve with more practice.

When you are reading material, solving issues, or making judgments in your daily life, try to use your critical thinking abilities. Gain knowledge of thinking and logic. You can learn about reasoning and logic from a variety of books and websites. Gaining knowledge about these subjects can improve your ability to think critically.

* Have an open mind. Being ready to examine all sides of an issue and maintaining an open mind are prerequisites for critical thinking. Stay away from making snap judgments and be open to changing your view in the face of fresh knowledge.

* Don't hesitate to pose inquiries. One of the best ways to challenge your own preconceptions and gain more knowledge about a subject is to ask questions.

Never hesitate to inquire, even if it seems foolish or apparent.

* Have the courage to think independently. To be critical, one must think independently and refrain from mindlessly adopting the viewpoints of others. Be prepared to question authority and establish your own ideas. The ability to think critically is crucial for success in the workplace, in school, and in life. You may become more adept at making decisions, solving problems, and communicating by engaging in critical thinking exercises. You can also develop personally and become more self-aware.

Being modest

It is impossible to exaggerate the value of humility. It is a necessary attribute for success in all facets of life.

Being humble allows us to be receptive to growth and learning. We are prepared to acknowledge our mistakes and ask for assistance from others. We are more inclined to treat people with kindness and compassion. The virtue of humility has several advantages. People with humility have a higher chance of succeeding in their jobs. It is more probable that they maintain close bonds with their friends and family. Additionally, those who are humble tend to be happier and more satisfied with their lives.

Humility may be developed in a variety of ways. Mindfulness practice is one method. The practice of mindfulness involves focusing attention on the current moment without passing judgment.

Being attentive increases our awareness of our feelings, thoughts, and behaviors. We are also more conscious of other people's feelings, ideas, and behaviors. Being more mindful of this can make us more kind and modest. Gratitude practice is another technique to develop humility. Being grateful for the blessings in our lives is the practice of gratitude. Being thankful makes it easier for us to concentrate on the good things in our lives. This may encourage us to be more grateful and modest about what we have. Finally, by forgiving others, we can develop humility. The act of forgiving someone involves letting go of grudges and animosity. We are letting go of the past and moving forward when we forgive people. This may encourage us to accept and be more modest toward other people.

A strong trait that may help us in every aspect of our lives is humility. It is a trait that every one of us ought to work to develop.

Here are some instances of how humility may benefit you in your life:

* Being humble can help you be more receptive to criticism and to learning from your errors in the workplace. It might also support you in forging solid bonds with your coworkers. Being humble in your personal life might make you more tolerant and understanding of other people. You may also find that it makes you happier with your life. Being humble in your relationships might help you treat your spouse with greater consideration and respect.

Additionally, it can make dispute resolution more skillful for you. All things considered, humility is a trait that will help you in every aspect of your life. It's a trait you ought to work to develop.

Here are some pointers for developing humility:

* Stay receptive to criticism. When you receive comments from someone, try to have an open mind and consider things from their point of view.

* Own up to your errors. Errors are to be expected. Acknowledging your errors and growing from them are crucial.

* Show sympathy, gratitude and kindness. Consider how you would like to be treated.

Be grateful for all the blessings in your life, no matter how minor. Pardon both others and yourself. It's human nature to make errors; therefore, extend forgiveness to both yourself and other people. Being modest is a process rather than a final goal. You have to put effort into it each and every day. However, it's worthwhile. Being humble will improve both your life and yourself as a person.

The importance of lifelong learning

People have debated the benefits of lifelong learning for ages. It is more crucial than ever to keep learning and developing in a world that is changing so quickly nowadays.

* Increased knowledge and abilities: Learning throughout your life gives you the opportunity to pick up new skills and information that will assist both your personal and professional lives. * Enhanced cognitive function: Keeping your mind active and your memory sharp can be achieved by learning new things.

* Greater work satisfaction: Lifelong learners are more likely to have contented employment.

* Lessened tension: Developing new skills can aid in lowering anxiety and stress levels.

* Enhanced social skills: Continuing education can facilitate networking and friend-making.

* Enhanced self-confidence: Acquiring new skills can boost your self-assurance and competence. Lifelong learning may take many different forms. You can converse with others who are more knowledgeable than you are, read books, view instructional videos, or enroll in classes. Finding a hobby or pastime that you are interested in and ready to stick with is crucial.

Here are some pointers for beginning lifelong learning:

* Establish goals: What do you want to learn? Which competencies are you hoping to gain? Planning how to get there may begin as soon as you have a clear idea of what you want to accomplish.

* Locate a mentor: A mentor may offer direction and encouragement as you set out on your path of lifelong learning.

* Make a commitment: Learning for a lifetime requires time and work. Be ready to dedicate yourself to regularly learning new things.

* Have patience: Acquiring new skills requires time. If you don't notice results right away, don't give up.

* Reward yourself: Make sure to acknowledge and celebrate your accomplishments as you move closer to your lifetime learning objectives. You'll be able to stay motivated and on course by doing this. An important element of a happy and healthy existence is lifelong learning.

You can stay on top of your job, enhance your relationships, and have a richer, more fulfilling life if you keep learning and developing.

SECTION TWO

Casting Doubt on Assumptions

What do you mean by assumptions?

Beliefs we have about the world, even in the absence of proof, are called assumptions. Our experiences, our culture, or our own prejudices may all be the basis for them. Though they might be useful in helping us make sense of the world, assumptions can sometimes create blunders.

When we form assumptions, we use our own beliefs to fill in the knowledge gaps. When we don't have all the knowledge we need, this might be useful, but it can also cause us to draw the wrong conclusions.

For instance, you can be mistaken if you believe that someone is furious only because they are frowning. They might be frowning as a means of focus or as a sign of discomfort.

Assumptions might influence how we behave toward other people. You might be less inclined to listen to someone if you think that just because they speak with an accent, they are not bright. This could be detrimental to the other individual as well as to you.

It's critical to recognize and challenge our presumptions. Our lives shouldn't be dictated by our presumptions. We ought to be receptive to fresh insights and viewpoints.

We have to be open to having our opinions changed in response to fresh information.

We are less likely to assume when we are aware of what we do not know. We are more inclined to look for information and ask inquiries. We tend to be more receptive to novel concepts. We are more likely to be flexible in our thinking.

Being aware of your ignorance is a useful skill. It may contribute to your increased success in life. You may be able to forge stronger bonds with others. It can support your growth and learning. It might make you a better person.

The following advice can help you become more conscious of your assumptions:

* Be mindful of your ideas. When you find yourself passing judgment on someone or anything, consider whether you have any supporting data.

* Make an effort to find out about the experiences and backgrounds of new people you meet. Make an effort to take the author's viewpoint into account when you read anything.

* Be open to having your mind changed. Be prepared to revise your opinions if fresh knowledge challenges your presumptions.

* Have humility. Never forget that there is always more to learn and that you don't know everything.

Learning what you do not know is an ongoing process. It is a worthwhile adventure to go on.

Why does it matter what assumptions are made?

It matters because they help us make sense of the world around us, assumptions are crucial. They assist us in making forecasts about the future and completing the information gaps. We may also utilize assumptions to inform our judgments and direct our activities.

Assumptions, nevertheless, can sometimes be harmful. We risk making bad judgments if we base our assumptions on unsupported information. It's critical to recognize our presumptions and have the courage to challenge them.

Acquiring evidence to bolster our assumptions is one technique to ensure their accuracy. We can do this by carrying out studies, consulting specialists, or just paying attention to the environment. Following the collection of evidence, we may assess our hypotheses to ensure their continued validity.

Being conscious of the biases that may affect our presumptions is also crucial. Everybody has biases, which are thought patterns that might cause us to form incorrect conclusions. Confirmation bias, the propensity to look for evidence to support our preexisting ideas, and the availability heuristic, the propensity to assess the likelihood of an occurrence depending on how quickly instances come to mind, are two examples of prevalent biases.

We may reduce the influence of our prejudices on our presumptions by being conscious of them. We may do this by looking for material that contradicts our opinions, taking into account different viewpoints, and keeping an open mind about the potential that we could be mistaken.

In life, assumptions are unavoidable. They assist us in understanding the environment we live in.

Make choices. But it's critical to recognize our presumptions and be open to challenging them. We can reduce the possibility of making bad judgments by doing this.

The following are some real-world instances where assumptions are employed:

* Based on their looks, their body language, and their speech, people often form snap judgments about their personalities when you first meet them.

* When attempting to address a problem, assumptions are made about the nature of the issue and potential fixes.

* As you consider your options, you inevitably make assumptions about how things could turn out.

Although assumptions can be useful in a variety of circumstances, they can also result in miscommunication and other issues.

It's critical to recognize your presumptions and have the courage to challenge them. You may avoid basing judgments on false information by doing this.

The following advice can help you steer clear of assumptions:

Recognize your own prejudices. Everybody has biases, which are mental models that might cause us to form false conclusions. Confirmation bias—the propensity to look for evidence to support our already-held beliefs—and the availability heuristic—the propensity to assess the likelihood of an occurrence depending on how quickly instances spring to mind—are two examples of prevalent biases.

* Remain receptive to fresh knowledge that may refute your presumptions when making decisions.

* Be open to having your mind changed. Be prepared to revise your opinions if fresh knowledge challenges your presumptions.

* Make sure you communicate in a clear and straightforward manner. When interacting with people, use language that is succinct and straightforward. This will assist in preventing miscommunications.

* Make inquiries. Ask for inquiries if you have any doubts about something. This will assist you in learning more and preventing preconceptions.

How can we recognize our presumptions?

Asking yourself what you believe you know is a simple technique to discover your preconceptions. What do you think the world is like? What views do you have on certain subjects? You may begin challenging your assumptions once you've compiled a list of them. Do they actually exist? Exist any more plausible explanations?

Observing how you speak might also help you recognize your presumptions. Do you employ phrases like "never," "always," and "everyone"? These phrases may indicate that you are assuming something. If you say, "I always get a headache when I eat chocolate".

For instance, you are making the assumption that chocolate is the reason you get headaches. Still, other variables, like thirst or stress, can be at play.

You may begin to question your assumptions after you've recognized them. Consider whether there is any data to back up your presumptions. If not, you might have to reconsider. Though it might be challenging to alter your perspective, it's crucial to have an open mind to fresh knowledge.

Being aware of your ignorance is a really useful skill that may enhance your life in a variety of ways. It can assist you in learning new things, becoming more receptive to new ideas, and making better judgments.

Thus, the next time you catch yourself assuming anything, stop and consider your assumptions. You could be taken aback by what you discover.

Here are some more pointers to help you recognize your assumptions:

Be mindful of your ideas. What's on your mind? What presumptions do you have?

Be mindful of the words you use. Do you employ phrases like "never," "always," and "everyone"? These phrases may indicate that you are assuming something.

Pose inquiries to yourself. What am I aware of on this subject? What am I ignorant of? What presumptions do I have?

Engage in conversation. Find out what they believe about the subject. What presumptions do they have?

Conduct research. Examine relevant books, articles, and websites. What details are you able to obtain?

How can we question the assumptions we make?

The capacity to remain receptive to novel concepts and information, as well as to modify one's opinions in response to data that challenges preconceived notions, is known as "knowing what one doesn't know." It is essential to both lifelong learning and critical thinking.

There are several approaches to refuting our presumptions. To start with, just be conscious of them. Being conscious of our presumptions allows us to start challenging them and determining their veracity. We can converse with those who have different opinions than us and look for knowledge that challenges our presumptions.

Using metacognition in our practice is another approach to questioning our preconceptions. The capacity to reflect on our own thoughts is known as metacognition. We can begin to see our assumptions for what they are—just assumptions—when we engage in metacognitive reflection on them. We can also begin to notice how our actions and thoughts may be influenced by our presumptions.

By keeping an open mind to fresh experiences, we may refute our presumptions. We are compelled to face our preconceptions about the world when we attempt new activities. We may discover that the world is larger than we initially believed or that our presumptions are incorrect.

Although it's not always simple, questioning our presumptions is crucial to learning and development. We create space for fresh possibilities when we question our presumptions. We are open to new experiences, new people, and new lessons. We can also develop greater tolerance and openness toward other people.

There are several things you can do to refute your presumptions.

Be conscious of your presumptions first. What do you think is real? Why do you think that?

Look for data that defies your presumptions. View films, read books, and read articles that contradict your ideas.

Converse with others whose opinions differ from your own. Pay attention to their viewpoints and make an effort to comprehend the reasons behind their beliefs.

Have an open mind to new things. Explore new horizons, make new friends, and visit unfamiliar locations.

It may be challenging, but also very beneficial, to question your preconceptions.

It can support your own development and make you more accepting and understanding of other people. So begin now if you want to question your presumptions!

Here are some more pointers to help you question your presumptions:

* Have the humility to acknowledge your mistakes. It's OK to have second thoughts after learning new knowledge.

* Never discount something because it contradicts your beliefs.

* Show regard for the beliefs of others. You may respect someone's right to believe what they want, even if you don't agree with them.

* Be prepared to engage in challenging dialogue. You will need to have some difficult conversations if you wish to question someone's presumptions.

* Have patience. Changing your preconceptions takes time. Don't anticipate seeing outcomes right away.

* Have perseverance. If you don't notice results immediately, don't give up. You will ultimately notice improvement if you continue to challenge your preconceptions.

Putting your presumptions to the test is a lifetime endeavor. It's something you ought to be focusing on all the time. You will become more accepting and tolerant the more you question your preconceptions. You will also be a better person if you are more accepting and open-minded.

How do we go over our presumptions?

Beliefs we have about the world, even in the absence of proof, are known as assumptions. They may be derived from our culture, our prior experiences, or just what we have been told. In certain situations, assumptions might be useful, but they can also produce blunders.

Being more conscious of our presumptions is one way to overcome them. This may be achieved by keeping an eye on our thoughts and identifying any assumptions we make. We may begin to challenge our presumptions once we become conscious of them. We may examine if our assumptions are supported by any evidence and if there are any alternative plausible explanations for the things we are assuming.

Being receptive to fresh knowledge is another strategy for dispelling our presumptions. We may do this by reading various points of view, seeing new locations, and listening to the opinions of others. Exposure to novel knowledge can assist us in questioning our preconceptions and developing fresh perspectives on the world.

By having the flexibility to reconsider our positions, we can get over our presumptions. Though it might be challenging, it's critical to keep in mind that our preconceptions are just that—assumptions. They're not always correct, and they're not facts.

By being open to changing our opinions in response to new facts, we may steer clear of blunders and lead more enlightened lives.

The following are some instances where errors might result from assumptions:

* You may act in a way that really enrages someone if you imagine they are upset with you.

* You might not even attempt anything if you believe you're not very good at it.

* You might not even ask someone out on a date if you think they're going to reject you.

As evidenced by the following, assumptions may significantly affect our lives.

They may stop us from attempting new things, taking chances, and forming relationships with others. For this reason, it's critical to be conscious of our presumptions and to question them when appropriate.

The following advice can help you get past your presumptions:

* Be mindful of your thoughts and identify any assumptions you may be making.

* Consider if your assumptions are supported by any evidence and whether there are any other plausible explanations for the items you are assuming.

* Read various points of view, visit new locations, and pay attention to other people's opinions.

* Keep in mind that your presumptions remain only that—presumptions. They're not always correct, and they're not facts. You may avoid making mistakes and lead a more enlightened life if you're prepared to have your opinions changed in response to fresh facts.

SECTION THREE

Having an open mind to fresh concepts

The value of having an open mind to new concepts

One cannot stress how crucial it is to be receptive to new concepts. It is more crucial than ever to be able to adapt and pick up new skills in today's environment of constant change. We will soon fall behind if we are closed off to fresh ideas

Being receptive to new ideas is crucial for a variety of reasons. First of all, novel concepts can assist us in resolving issues that have been troubling us.

Seeing things from a different angle while we are stuck might be beneficial. We could make the breakthrough we require to proceed with a fresh concept.

Fresh perspectives can aid in our development. Our knowledge and comprehension of the world are continuously growing when we are receptive to new concepts. Both professional and personal progress may result from this.

Novel concepts can foster interpersonal relationships. We forge bonds with one another and foster a sense of community when we exchange ideas. Given how disconnected we are from one another in today's environment, this can be particularly crucial.

It goes without saying that being receptive to new ideas does not require us to concur with everything we hear. Critical thinking skills and the ability to assess novel concepts on their own merits are crucial. But we can never learn and develop if we are closed off to fresh ideas.

In conclusion, it is impossible to exaggerate the value of having an open mind to new concepts. We must be flexible and open to learning new things if we are to prosper in the modern world. The secret to both professional and personal progress is to be receptive to new ideas.

Here are some more perspectives on the significance of having an open mind to new concepts:

Novel concepts can provide us with fresh perspectives on the world. They can disprove our presumptions and aid in our understanding of various viewpoints.

* Creativity and innovation can result from new ideas. They can assist us in developing fresh approaches to issues as well as new goods and services.

* We can be motivated to act by novel concepts. They have the power to inspire us to transform our lives and the planet.

How to be more receptive to novel concepts

It may be challenging to keep up with the quick changes in the world. There are always new concepts to consider, and it may be challenging to decide which ones are worthwhile. Nonetheless, success in today's society depends on having an open mind to fresh concepts.

Being receptive to new ideas is crucial for a variety of reasons. Innovation might result from fresh concepts. We are more inclined to solve difficulties creatively when we are receptive to fresh ideas. Fresh perspectives can aid in our development. We are more likely to learn new things and broaden our perspective on the world when we are receptive to new ideas.

Novel concepts can foster interpersonal relationships. We are more likely to connect with others from diverse backgrounds when we are receptive to fresh ideas.

Openness to new ideas can be fostered in a variety of ways. Reading widely is one method. Reading introduces us to fresh viewpoints and concepts. Traveling is another way to increase your receptivity to new ideas. We encounter many cultures and lifestyles when we travel. Lastly, conversing with others who are different from us might help us become more receptive to new ideas. We are exposed to fresh viewpoints and ideas when we converse with people from diverse backgrounds.

It is not always simple to be receptive to fresh ideas. Letting go of our outdated ideas and perspectives can be challenging. But it's crucial to keep in mind that learning new concepts can advance our development. We may do great things if we are receptive to fresh ideas.

These pointers will help you be more receptive to novel concepts:

1. Be open to hearing other people's viewpoints. When someone shares a viewpoint that differs from your own, make an effort to listen to them without bias. Just because someone has a different perspective than you doesn't mean you have to agree with them.

2. Stay willing to try new things. You won't be exposed to novel concepts if you consistently engage in the same activities. Try to experiment with different foods, activities, and even ways of thinking.

3. Show curiosity. The secret to learning and development is curiosity. Curiosity about the world around you makes you more inclined to look for fresh knowledge and concepts.

4. Show modesty. It's critical to acknowledge your limitations as a knowledge base. There's always someone who knows more than you do, and there's always something new to learn. Even if someone is younger or less experienced than you, have an open mind and try to learn from them.

5. Be open to having your mind changed. Be prepared to have your opinions changed if fresh knowledge contradicts your preconceptions. It's OK to acknowledge your error. It's actually an indication of intelligence and power.

Being receptive to new ideas is a continuous process. You have to put effort into it each and every day. However, it's worthwhile. You will develop and learn more the more receptive you are to new concepts. You'll also be more successful in life as you develop and study.

The advantages of having a receptive mind

It is more crucial than ever to be receptive to new ideas in the rapidly evolving world of today.

New concepts that have the potential to completely transform the way we live and work are always appearing due to the speed at which technology is developing. We can remain ahead of the curve and make sure we are ready for the future by keeping an open mind to these fresh concepts.

Having an open mind to new concepts has several advantages. It can first aid in our learning and development. We are compelled to adopt new perspectives when we are exposed to novel concepts. This may enable us to gain fresh viewpoints and understandings. Secondly, we may become more creative by keeping an open mind to new concepts. We are more likely to solve difficulties creatively when we don't hesitate to attempt new things.

Third, having an open mind to new concepts can improve our professional achievement. Employers are searching for workers who can think creatively and unconventionally in the cutthroat employment market of today. We may improve our chances of success and become more marketable by being receptive to new ideas.

Of course, being receptive to new concepts is not without its difficulties. First of all, it might be hard to let go of outdated concepts. Everybody has their own set of values and beliefs, and it can be challenging to alter them in response to new facts. Second, there may occasionally be conflict when one is receptive to new ideas. Others may not always agree with us when we share our novel concepts with them.

Disagreements and even conflicts may result from this. Third, it might take time to be receptive to new concepts. Developing fresh viewpoints and conducting research on novel concepts takes time. If we're not careful, we may easily follow the newest fads and trends without truly giving them much thought.

The advantages of being receptive to novel concepts far exceed the drawbacks, notwithstanding the difficulties. We must be able to adapt and develop in a world that is changing all the time. We can make sure we're ready for the future by keeping an open mind to fresh concepts.

Here are some pointers for widening your mind to novel concepts:

* Show curiosity. Make inquiries and look for fresh data.

* Have an open mind. Accept new ideas with an open mind, even if they diverge from your own.

* Show tolerance. Recognize that others can think and behave differently than you do.

* Show adaptability. Be open to having your opinions changed in response to fresh information.

* Have a risk-taking mindset. Step outside of your comfort zone and try new things.

You may take advantage of the numerous advantages that come with fresh ideas and cultivate an open mind by implementing these suggestions.

The difficulties of becoming receptive to new concepts

For many people, it might be difficult to be receptive to new ideas. It may be hard to let go of our preconceived notions and ways of thinking, and it can be much harder to consider the possibility that we could be mistaken. Nonetheless, development and advancement depend on having an open mind to new concepts.

Being receptive to new ideas is crucial for a variety of reasons. First of all, novel concepts can assist us in resolving issues that have been troubling us.

Seeing things from a different angle while we are stuck might be beneficial. We can also get fresh perspectives on the world by embracing new ideas. They can refute our presumptions and convictions and advance our understanding of the outside world.

It's not always simple, of course, to be receptive to new ideas. Letting go of our outdated ideas and perspectives can be challenging. It can sometimes be hard to admit when we could be mistaken. But it's crucial to keep in mind that having an open mind about new concepts is a sign of strength rather than weakness. It demonstrates our willingness to develop and learn.

There are a few things you might do if you find it difficult to be receptive to new ideas. Try to become more conscious of your own prejudices first. Everybody has prejudices, and they might make it difficult for us to perceive things objectively. Secondly, let your thoughts be more flexible. This entails having an open mind to novel concepts, even when they diverge from your own. Lastly, strive to be more inquisitive. The secret to learning and development is curiosity. Being interested in the world around you increases your likelihood of being receptive to novel concepts.

It might be difficult to be receptive to new ideas, but it is an endeavor worth taking on. We make room for new possibilities when we are receptive to fresh perspectives.

We have the capacity to improve the world through learning and development.

Here are some more ideas about the difficulties of having an open mind to new concepts:

* Letting go of our ingrained opinions and thought processes can be challenging. These opinions might be firmly embedded in our identities and have been held for a very long period of time. Changing our thoughts may be frightening, and we can be concerned about what other people would think of us if we did.

* Admitting we may be mistaken can be challenging. Everyone likes to believe that they are capable and bright.

Admitting we don't know everything and that we might need to pick up knowledge from others might be humility.

* Managing uncertainty may be challenging. We accept the chance that we may be mistaken when we are receptive to fresh perspectives. Since we may not appreciate the concept of not knowing everything, this might be a frightening proposition.

* Changing our behavior might be challenging. It might be hard to stop a habit after we've established one. This is particularly true if we have been engaging in the behavior for a considerable amount of time.

SECTION FOUR

Thinking in a distinct way

Imagination is the capacity to generate fresh, original thoughts. It is the capacity to think creatively and from an alternative point of view. Being able to think differently is an important life skill that will benefit you in both your professional and personal interactions.

You may cultivate your capacity to think differently in a variety of ways. To start, try brainstorming a little. The goal of the brainstorming technique is to produce as many ideas as you can, regardless of how absurd or unreal they may sound.

After you've compiled a list of ideas, you can begin to assess each one to determine which is most practical.

Reading books and articles about innovation and creativity is another way to strengthen your capacity for unconventional thought. You can learn about various ways of thinking and how to implement them in your own life by using a variety of resources.

Finally, by just being more receptive to new ideas, you can also improve your capacity for unconventional thought. It is more likely that you will generate original ideas when you are receptive to new ones. Thus, be open to trying new things, getting to know new people, and seeing different cultures.

You will get more adept at thinking differently the more diverse viewpoints you are exposed to.

Reasons why an average person rethinking is challenging

Though transformational, rethinking is a difficult mental task that might be especially difficult for the typical individual. In this investigation, we examine the complex causes of the difficulties people have while trying to overcome ingrained mental habits. It is essential to comprehend these obstacles in order to create a mentality that is more flexible and open-minded.

Cognitive Comfort Zones: People are drawn to familiarity and comfort by nature.

People gradually create cognitive comfort zones, which are safe havens in their minds where they feel comfortable with the ideas and opinions they already hold. Rethinking necessitates moving outside of these comfort zones, which may cause resistance and pain.

Fear of Uncertainty: Rethinking frequently necessitates accepting ambiguity and uncertainty. A person's dread of the unknown may be crippling, preventing them from questioning their preconceived notions. The erratic character of reevaluation may conflict with the natural need for stability.

Social Conditioning: A person's perspective is greatly influenced by society. There is a reluctance to stray from accepted ideas because of the need to live up to social standards and expectations. The process of rethinking is made more difficult by having to navigate peer pressure, culture, and familial pressures.

Emotional Investment: People frequently have deep emotional connections with the ideas and viewpoints they hold. Rethinking necessitates facing these emotional commitments and maybe changing them, which can be a difficult and emotionally draining process.

Lack of Exposure to Diverse Perspectives: A person's perspective on the world may become more limited if they are not exposed to a wide range of experiences and points of view. Without exposure to a range of viewpoints, people might find it difficult to understand why rethinking is necessary or advantageous.

Time Restraints and Setting Priorities: The modern world places a lot of demands on people's time and attention, making life fast-paced. Rethinking necessitates setting aside time for reflection, study, and introspection—something that many people may not consider a luxury.

Here are a few advantages to adopting a different perspective:

It can assist you in problem-solving more skillfully.

It can assist you in generating fresh, creative ideas.

It may facilitate your increased creativity.

It may enable you to achieve greater professional success.

It can assist you in achieving greater success in your interpersonal interactions.

The benefits of thinking differently

The benefits of thinking differently are numerous. When you think differently, you are able to come up with new and innovative ideas. You are also able to see things from a different perspective, which can help you solve problems more effectively. Additionally, thinking differently can help you to be more creative and to come up with new ways of doing things.

One of the most important benefits of thinking differently is that it allows you to be more creative. When you think differently, you are able to come up with new and innovative ideas.

This may be beneficial in a variety of scenarios, such as when you are attempting to solve an issue or when you are trying to come up with a new product or service.

Another benefit of thinking differently is that it helps you see things from a new perspective. This may be beneficial in a variety of scenarios, such as when you are attempting to comprehend someone else's point of view or when you are trying to solve an issue. When you are able to see things from a new perspective, you are more likely to come up with a solution that is both successful and fair.

Thinking differently might help you be more adaptive. When you are able to think differently, you are more likely to be able to adapt to change.

This is a vital talent in today's environment, as change is continuous. When you are able to adapt to change, you are more likely to be successful in anything you do.

Here are some other strategies for thinking differently:

* Remain receptive to fresh perspectives. Don't be scared to attempt new things or to think about things from a fresh perspective.

* Have a risk-taking mindset. Don't be scared to fail.

* Have perseverance. Don't give up easily.

* Be optimistic. Have faith in your own abilities and your capacity for original thought.

How to adopt a different perspective

It is possible to learn and develop the ability to think in novel ways. It is the capacity to think beyond the box, to approach issues creatively, and to view things from fresh angles. Learning to think differently can be accomplished in a variety of ways. Mindfulness practice is one method. The practice of mindfulness involves focusing attention on the current moment without passing judgment. Being attentive allows you to notice your thoughts and emotions without becoming sucked into them. This might assist you in developing fresh thoughts and gaining new perspectives on things.

Developing your creative side is another approach to acquiring new ways of thinking.

The capacity to generate fresh, innovative ideas is what is known as creativity. There are several approaches to developing creativity, including mind mapping, free writing, and brainstorming. Being creative allows you to go beyond the box and provide ideas for solutions that others might not have thought about.

Studying various cultures and viewpoints might help you develop new ways of thinking. Learning about various cultures exposes you to fresh perspectives on the world and new ways of thinking. You may become more accepting of other people and have an open mind as a result of this.

One important talent that might help you thrive in life is the ability to think differently.

It can assist you in problem-solving, idea generation, and creativity. There are many tools out there if you want to learn how to think in a different way. You may work on your creativity, mindfulness, and cross-cultural knowledge. With practice, you may learn to think differently and to perceive the world from a different perspective.

Here are some more pointers for adopting a different way of thinking:

* Remain receptive to fresh perspectives. Try new things and adopt fresh perspectives on things without fear.

* Use your imagination. Never be scared to think creatively and unconventionally to generate fresh concepts.

* Have perseverance. Hold on to your resolve. Continue experimenting and adopting fresh perspectives until you arrive at a workable answer.

* Have patience. Learning to think differently takes time. Don't anticipate seeing outcomes right away.

* Have a good attitude. Have faith in your own abilities to change the way you think.

SECTION FIVE

How to get beyond barriers to adopting a fresh perspective

1. Stay receptive to fresh perspectives. The greatest barrier to adopting a fresh perspective is our own narrow-mindedness. We frequently oppose change and have a tendency to cling to what we know and are comfortable with. However, we must be receptive to novel concepts, even if they appear unusual or foreign, if we are to be able to think creatively.

2. Have a risk-taking mindset. Taking chances is frequently necessary to think differently. We might have to take risks, venture outside of our comfort zones, and possibly fail.

We will never be able to overcome our ingrained beliefs if we are unwilling to take chances.

3. Remain tenacious. Differentiating oneself is not always easy. It requires practice, patience, and work. There will be moments when we experience frustration, discouragement, and a sense of stagnation. But if we keep at it, we'll eventually get over these challenges and begin to think in new ways.

4. Use your imagination. It takes imagination to think in novel ways. We must possess the ability to generate original ideas, approach challenges in novel ways, and adopt fresh viewpoints on the world. We can change the way we think if we unleash our creative potential.

5. Exude confidence. Our own self-doubt stands in the way of thinking differently in many cases. We might not think we're capable of thinking in a new way, or we could be worried about what other people might think if we did. But we must have faith in our own skills if we hope to get over these challenges.

We'll have no trouble getting beyond the challenges of adopting a new way of thinking if we can adhere to these suggestions. And once we can think in new ways, we'll be able to solve issues in novel ways, generate fresh ideas, and adopt fresh viewpoints on the world. They will all contribute to our increased success in life.

Here are some more pointers for getting past barriers to adopting a new way of thinking:

* Examine your presumptions. Our own presumptions are one of the main barriers to adopting new ways of thinking. Assumptions about the world we live in are common, and they might impede our capacity for original thought. We must be open to exploring alternative options and prepared to question our preconceptions in order to get over this barrier.

* Be open to being corrected. We also need to overcome our fear of being incorrect in order to think differently. Most of the time, we want to be correct because we fear that if we're not, we'll be viewed as foolish or unable.

However, we must be prepared to be mistaken if we wish to adopt a different perspective. We must be prepared to try new things and take chances, even if it means making errors.

* Acquire knowledge from others. Studying the thoughts of others is one of the finest methods for developing new ways of thinking. Examine publications and books on innovation and creativity. Speak with others who hold differing opinions from your own. Additionally, take note of the environment you live in and how others handle challenges.

* Get in shape. It takes work to think differently, just like everything else. You'll get more proficient at it with more practice.

Therefore, if you don't notice results right away, don't give up. If you practice consistently, you will ultimately begin to notice improvements.

The future of alternative ways of thinking

The issue of thinking differently in the future has been studied by a wide range of individuals, including philosophers, scientists, and artists. Though there are a few broad patterns that can be seen, the future of thinking differently is not something that can be definitively predicted.

The growing significance of creativity and innovation is one trend that is probably going to stick around in the future.

The ability to think creatively and unconventionally is more crucial than ever in a world where things are changing all the time. People will need to be able to think differently and be receptive to new ideas in order to achieve this.

The growing significance of collaboration is another trend that will probably not go away in the near future. Being able to collaborate and exchange ideas with others is more crucial than ever in a world where everything is connected. People will need to be able to think in new ways and be receptive to other viewpoints in order to do this.

The creation of new technology will probably influence the way that people think in the future.

Artificial intelligence and virtual reality are two examples of new technologies that are already altering the way we think and interact with the outside world. These technologies will probably keep altering the way we learn and think in the future.

All things considered, the era of thinking differently is probably going to witness a lot of innovation and development. People will need to be more imaginative, cooperative, and receptive to fresh perspectives in the future. It will also be a period in which advances in technology will persist in altering our cognitive and educational processes.

Here are some concrete instances of how adopting a fresh perspective now might prove advantageous later on:

* Thinking differently at work may produce fresh, creative ideas that support the growth of companies.

* In the classroom, adopting a new way of thinking may foster more innovative and successful learning.

* Having an alternative way of thinking can improve communication and strengthen bonding between people in intimate relationships.

* Thinking outside the box when tackling challenges can lead to innovative and practical solutions.

CONCLUSION

Finally, "Rethink Revolution: Unleashing the Power of Fresh Perspective" challenges readers to set out on a life-changing path of reflection and development. Through questioning the status quo and appreciating the energy of new viewpoints, the book encourages both individual and group growth. It emphasizes how crucial it is to challenge presumptions, adjust to change, and draw strength from uncharted areas of knowledge. The need to reevaluate becomes both a revolutionary act and an essential talent for handling uncertainty as we make our way through the complexity of our quickly changing environment.

The ability to reflect, grow, and adjust enables people to prosper in a constantly shifting environment, encouraging creativity, resiliency, and a better comprehension of both the outside world and oneself. "Rethink Revolution" paves the path for a more enlightened and flexible future by serving as a guide for individuals prepared to explore unexplored areas of thinking and realize their full potential.